Sauces & Marinades

STEP-BY-STEP

Sauces & Marinades

Nicola Diggins

Photographs by James Duncan

INDEX

First published in 1995 by Lorenz Books

© 1995 Anness Publishing Limited
Lorenz Books is an imprint of
Anness Publishing Limited
Boundary Row Studios
1 Boundary Row
London SE1 8HP

ISBN 1 85967 098 9

A CIP catalogue record is available from the British Library.

Publisher: Joanna Lorenz
Project Editor: Joanne Rippin
Designer: Kim Bale, Visual Image
Jacket Designer: Alan Marshall
Photographer:James Duncan

Typeset by MC Typeset Ltd, Rochester, Kent

MEASUREMENTS
Three sets of equivalent measurements have been provided in the recipes here, in the following
order: Metric, Imperial and American. It is essential that units of measurement are not mixed
within each recipe. Where conversions result in awkward numbers, these have been rounded for
convenience, but are still accurate enough to produce successful results.

Printed and bound in Hong Kong

CONTENTS

INTRODUCTION

Culinary life would be very dull without sauces. Plainly cooked food is all very well and makes a pleasant change after a spate of overindulgence, but it can become decidedly monotonous. In earlier times, before refrigerators, unadorned food was in all probability vaguely unpleasant, which is no doubt why sauces have a long history in nearly every culture known for its cuisine.

A sauce is generally soft and flowing, although there are exceptions; it should be rich and concentrated in flavour, not harsh but well-rounded and mellow. In other words the sauce may be thin but the flavour shouldn't be! It should enhance the food it is served with but shouldn't overpower it. Equally, serve a generous measure, but don't leave the food swimming. It's good to know what exactly it is you're eating.

A sauce may be an essential part of a dish, like those from the marinade chapter. In these, the flavours blend so well that you're hardly aware of the sauce at all. Or it may be served as an accompaniment, in which case you have a free rein, especially with the more subtly flavoured meats, fish and vegetables. Some sauces are traditionally served with specific foods and many of the classic sauces fall within this category: bigarade with duck, and tartare with fried fish, for instance. Although they could be served with other things, horseradish is a must with roast beef and, likewise, apple sauce with pork.

Fast gaining in popularity are salsas. They are very simple to make and unlike other sauces are crisp and crunchy in texture. They are ideal served with summer meals and barbecues when the ingredients they're made with are full of flavour. So if you're looking for variety with your meals, sauces cover everything!

Spices and Flavourings

Whereas herbs are generally the leaf parts of a plant, spices may be made from the seeds, bark, stems or roots. They are usually dried and may be sold whole or ground. As with herbs, keep them in airtight jars in a dark cupboard, particularly ground spices which loose their flavour more quickly than their whole counterparts. For the fullest flavour buy in small quantities and use up quickly.

Capers
These give a piquant note and are particularly good with fish.

Cardamoms
These oval, light green pods are very aromatic. They can be used whole or the seeds removed and crushed for a warm spicy flavour.

Chillies and Cayenne
Fresh and dried chillies add heat and vary according to size and colour. Generally, but not always, large, pale green chillies will be milder than small red ones. Dried chillies are always hotter than fresh. Cayenne is a very hot chilli. Wash your hands thoroughly after preparing chillies and if possible wear thin rubber gloves.

Cinnamon sticks
This is the sweetly flavoured rolled bark of a tropical evergreen tree. It can be bought ground, but the sticks give a mellow flavour to syrups and are easily removed.

Cloves
The plump, dried flower buds from an evergreen tree. They are aromatic with a faint bitter taste.

Coriander seeds
A sweet, warm aromatic spice, also available ground.

Garlic
A strongly flavoured member of the onion family, and should therefore be used in moderation. For less a pungent flavour, increase the cooking time. The pinky-purple cloves are considered to have a better flavour than the white varieties.

Ginger, fresh and dried
Fresh root ginger is the plump bulbous rhizome of the ginger plant. It is knobbly and should be peeled thinly with a potato peeler or sharp knife and chopped or grated. It has a hot, sharp, fresh taste quite different from ground ginger which is hot and peppery.

Juniper berries
These small purply-black berries have a sweet resinous aroma which can be released by crushing with a heavy-bladed knife before use.

Lemon grass
The bulbous base of this lemon-scented grass is usually used. It can be crushed and used whole or chopped for a stronger flavour.

Mace
This is the thin lacy cover of the nutmeg seed and has a similar, though more gentle, flavour. It is sold ground although whole mace is sometimes available.

Mustard
Comes as brown, black or white seed as well as traditional mustard powder, ground mustard seed blended with turmeric. It is a great flavour enhancer for cheese and egg sauces but should be used in moderation as it can be hot.

Nutmeg
Is the ripened dried seed of a large tropical tree. It has a rich mellow flavour which is greatly enhanced if freshly grated.

Paprika
A sweet, piquant spice, ideal for enhancing the flavour of vegetables and meat.

Peppercorns
Pepper is a universal seasoning. Dried black and white peppercorns are best freshly ground for the most pungency. Green peppercorns are available fresh, bottled in brine or dried.

Saffron
This is the dried thread-like stigma of a crocus. It gives a rich golden yellow colour and slightly musty sweet flavour to sauces.

Shallots
These are another member of the onion family and have a strong but more mellow flavour than the ordinary onion.

Turmeric
Like saffron, turmeric also gives a rich yellow colour to any sauce. Use in moderation as too much will leave an acrid bitter taste.

Vanilla pod
Used whole for a rich flavour.

nutmeg

green cardamoms

cayenne

juniper berries

mace

saffron

dried ginger

chilli

fresh root ginger

turmeric

coriander seeds

shallots

cloves

capers

green chilli

red chillies

mustard

lemon grass

black peppercorns

paprika

cinnamon sticks

green peppercorns

vanilla pod

garlic

Herbs

Herbs are simply edible plants whose leaves have a particularly strong flavour or aroma when they are crushed or heated. It is usual to use just the leaves stripped from coarse stalks, but occasionally softer stalks and flowers are used too.

By far the best way to use herbs is straight from the garden. You'll find they can be grown in a comparatively small area and given a sunny position most will thrive on poor soils or, failing that, pot a few up and stand on a brightly lit window-sill. Supermarkets now offer an increasing selection of pot-grown or prepacked fresh herbs. These are fine, especially out of season when there is little available from the garden; however, they can be soft and do not have the robust flavour of a freshly-picked garden crop.

Dried herbs are also useful in winter but a number lose their flavour and acquire hay-like overtones during drying and storage. Choose freeze-dried brands for the best flavour and store in airtight containers in a dark cupboard. Glass jars on a brightly lit spice rack may look attractive but are not ideal for the purpose.

Bay
Has dark green, leathery leaves which are generally used whole to impart a delicate flavour to sauces. To increase the flavour crush the leaf in your hand or tear into pieces. It is an essential component of a bouquet garni.

Chervil
A very delicate herb with soft, lacy, fern-like leaves. It has a very mild aniseed flavour so use plenty of it and only add near the end of cooking.

Chives
These have slender, cylindrical, grass-like leaves with a mild onion flavour. Use fresh with egg and cheese dishes.

Coriander
Coriander, with its finely scalloped broad leaf, has a spicy flavour. Leaves and stalks can be used, particularly fresh in salsas. It is essential in Indian dishes.

Dill
A distinctive, pungent herb with blue-green feathery leaves. It goes well with fish and egg dishes and also cream sauces.

Mint
Well known for its freshly flavoured, bright green leaves. Traditionally used with lamb, it is also good with fish and some vegetable dishes.

Oregano and marjoram
These herbs are from the same family. They both have small, oval, peppery-flavoured leaves which enhance tomato-based sauces. Oregano has a more robust flavour than sweeter marjoram.

Parsley
Two varieties of this widely-used herb are available, curly parsley and flat-leaf parsley. Flat-leaf parsley has a more concentrated flavour but curly parsley is more easily chopped. If using parsley in a marinade, stock or bouquet garni, use most of the stalk as this has a more concentrated flavour.

Rosemary
Rosemary has aromatic needle-like leaves. They are coarse and pungent so use sparingly and chop very finely.

Tarragon
With its long, narrow, glossy leaves and warm, aniseed flavour tarragon is an essential sauce flavouring. Use fresh French tarragon rather than Russian or dried tarragon.

Thyme
This herb has tiny oval leaves with a strong flavour and goes well with most dishes. Some varieties have a lemon scent which goes well with chicken and fish dishes. It is coarse, so remove the leaves from the stalks.

flat-leaf parsley

tarragon

parsley

chives

dill

chervil

mint

coriander

thyme

rosemary

oregano

bay

marjoram

Stocks

Many sauces depend for their depth and richness on a good quality stock base. Fresh stock will give the most balanced flavor and it is worth the effort to make it at home. It may be frozen successfully for several months. Canned beef bouillon and chicken broth are good substitutes. For everyday cooking, most cooks will use stock cubes, but these often have a salt base so taste carefully and season lightly.

FISH STOCK

INGREDIENTS
any fish bones, skin and
 trimmings available
1 onion
1 carrot
1 celery stalk
6 black peppercorns
2 bay leaves
3 stalks parsley

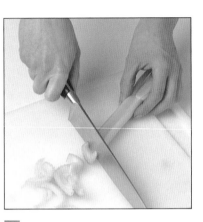

1 Peel and coarsely slice the onion. Peel and chop the carrot, and scrub and slice the celery.

2 Place all the ingredients in a large saucepan and add enough water to cover. Bring to a boil, skim the surface and simmer uncovered for 20 minutes.

3 Strain and use immediately or store for two days in the refrigerator.

BROWN STOCK

INGREDIENTS
2 tbsp vegetable oil
3 lb shin, shank or neck of beef
 bones, cut into pieces
8 oz shin of beef, cut into pieces
bouquet garni
2 onions, trimmed and quartered
2 carrots, scrubbed and chopped
2 celery sticks, sliced
1 tsp black peppercorns
$^{1}/_{2}$ tsp salt

1 Drizzle the vegetable oil over the bottom of a roasting pan, add the bones and meat. Coat in oil and bake at 425°F for 25–30 minutes or until well browned, turning regularly during cooking.

2 Transfer the meat and bones to a large saucepan, add the remaining ingredients and cover with 14 cups of water. Bring to the boil, skim the surface, then partially cover and simmer for $2^{1}/_{2}$–3 hours or until reduced to 7 cups.

3 Strain the stock into a bowl. Cool and remove the solidified fat before use. Store for up to 4 days in the refrigerator.

CHICKEN OR WHITE STOCK

INGREDIENTS
1 onion
4 cloves
1 carrot
2 leeks
2 celery sticks
1 chicken carcass, cooked or raw,
    or 750 g/1¹/₂ lb veal bones cut
    into pieces
bouquet garni
8 black peppercorns
2.5 ml/¹/₂ tsp salt

1 Peel the onion, cut into quarters and spike each quarter with a clove. Scrub and roughly chop the vegetables.

2 Break up the chicken carcass and place in a large saucepan with the remaining ingredients.

3 Cover with 1.7 litres/3 pints/7 cups water. Bring to the boil, skim the surface and simmer, partially covered for 2 hours. Strain the stock into a bowl and allow to cool. When cold remove the hardened fat before using. Store for up to 4 days in the refrigerator.

VEGETABLE STOCK

INGREDIENTS
30 ml/2 tbsp vegetable oil
1 onion
2 carrots
2 large celery sticks, plus any
    small amounts from the
    following: leeks, celeriac,
    parsnip, turnip, cabbage or
    cauliflower trimmings,
    mushrooms peelings
bouquet garni
6 black peppercorns

1 Peel, halve and slice the onion. Roughly chop the remaining vegetables.

2 Heat the oil in a large pan and fry the onion and vegetables until soft and lightly browned. Add the remaining ingredients and cover with 1.7 litres/3 pints/7 cups water.

3 Bring to the boil, skim the surface then partially cover and simmer for 1¹/₂ hours. Strain the stock and allow to cool. Store in the refrigerator for 2–3 days.

Thickening a Sauce

The simplest way to turn a liquid into a richer, more delicious sauce is to reduce it by bringing to a rolling boil over a high heat. However, there are many other methods, depending on the ingredients used in the dish you are cooking.

ROUX BASES

A roux, flour cooked gently in butter or oil, is the most common method of thickening. Generally equal quantities of butter and flour are used and the length of cooking time determines the type of sauce produced.

Roux blanc

Roux blond

Roux brun

ROUX BLANC

Melt the butter slowly then quickly stir in the flour. Continue cooking over a low heat for 1-2 minutes before removing from the heat and gradually adding hot liquid. This method will produce a white sauce.

ROUX BLOND

Made in the same way but the flour and butter are cooked for 3-4 minutes until they turn a pale straw colour.

ROUX BRUN

Again the butter and flour are cooked, but this time for 7-8 minutes until a pale nut brown colour. Stir continuously as it will easily burn.

BEURRE MANIÉ

If you have an unknown quantity of liquid to thicken, perhaps the liquid left over from a casserole or pot roast, then this method is ideal. Equal quantities of flour and butter are blended together, then small pea-sized pieces are stirred into the hot liquid, brought back to the boil and stirred until thickened.

Beurre manié

CORNFLOUR

A fine chalky flour ground from maize, 15 ml/1 tbsp will thicken 300 ml/$\frac{1}{2}$ pint of liquid. Blend the cornflour to a paste with 30 ml/2 tbsp of cold water then stir into the hot liquid and cook for 1-2 minutes until thickened.

cornflour

ARROWROOT

A powdery starch derived from the roots of the maranta plant. Used in a similar way to cornflour it will give a clearer sauce. Remove from the heat as soon as it thickens as it can be unstable.

arrowroot

EGG YOLKS AND CREAM

Blended egg yolks and cream make a rich sauce. Two egg yolks blended with 45-60 ml/3-4 tbsp of cream will thicken 300 ml/$\frac{1}{2}$ pint of liquid. Stir a little hot sauce into the egg and cream mixture then return to the rest of the liquid. Stir over a gentle heat until the sauce coats the back of a spoon. For extra care, cook in a double boiler or in a bowl over a saucepan of hot water.

egg yolks and cream

Keeping Sauces Warm

There is nothing more unappetizing than a congealed sauce, so keeping sauces warm successfully is essential. It can sometimes be tricky: the more delicate cream- and butter-based sauces curdle easily, whilst flour-based sauces may thin with prolonged heating. Follow the advice below to prevent a skin forming whilst keeping the sauce at a reasonable temperature.

1 Pour the sauce into a double boiler or a bowl suspended over a pan of hot, not boiling, water. To prevent a skin forming on a cream and butter sauce, cover the surface of the sauce with buttered greaseproof paper or clearfilm.

COOK'S TIP
All these types of sauces can also be kept warm in a vacuum flask. Make sure the flask is reasonably new and free of any stains or lingering smells. You may find that keeping the sauce in a flask alters its flavour, so this method should only be used as a last resort. Remember to heat the flask first with boiling water before gently pouring in the warm sauce.

2 For flour-based sauces, spoon over a little melted butter.

3 For sweet sauces, sprinkle the surface with caster sugar.

Bread Sauce

Smooth and surprisingly delicate, this old-fashioned sauce is traditionally served with roast chicken, turkey and game birds. If you'd prefer a less strong flavor, reduce the number of cloves and add a little freshly grated nutmeg instead.

Serves 6

INGREDIENTS
4 cloves
1 small onion
bay leaf
1¼ cup milk
2 cups fresh white breadcrumbs
1 tbsp butter
1 tbsp light cream
salt and pepper

milk

breadcrumbs

cloves

cream

onion

butter

bay leaf

I Peel the onion and stick the cloves into it. Put it into a saucepan with the bay leaf and pour in the milk.

2 Bring to a boil then remove from the heat and steep for 15–20 minutes. Remove the bay leaf and onion.

3 Return to the heat and stir in the crumbs. Simmer for 4–5 minutes or until thick and creamy.

4 Stir in the butter and cream, then season to taste.

Horseradish Sauce

This light, creamy sauce has a piquant, peppery flavor that's spiced with just a hint of mustard. It is the classic accompaniment to roast beef, but is perfect, too, with herby sausages and grilled fish.

Serves 6

INGREDIENTS
3 in piece fresh horseradish
1 tbsp lemon juice
2 tsp sugar
½ tsp English mustard powder
⅔ cup heavy cream

cream

horseradish

mustard

caster sugar

lemon

1 Scrub and peel the horseradish.

2 Grate the horseradish as finely as you can.

3 Mix together the horseradish, lemon juice, sugar and mustard powder.

4 Whip the cream until it stands in soft peaks then gently fold in the horseradish mixture.

Apple Sauce

Really more of a condiment than a sauce, this tart puree is usually served cold or warm, rather than hot. It's typically served with rice, roast pork or duck, but is also good with cold meats and savory pies.

Serves 6

INGREDIENTS
8 oz tart cooking apples
2 tbsp water
thin strip lemon rind
1 tbsp butter
1-2 tbsp sugar

apples

water

lemon

sugar

1 Peel, core and slice the apples.

2 Place the apples in a saucepan with the water and lemon peel. Cook uncovered over a low heat until very soft, stirring occasionally.

3 Remove the lemon rind, then beat to a pulp with a spoon or press through a strainer.

4 Stir in the butter and then add sugar to taste.

Cranberry Sauce

This is the sauce for roast turkey, but don't just keep it for festive occasions. The vibrant color and tart taste are a perfect partner to any white roast meat, and it makes a great addition to a chicken sandwich.

Serves 6

INGREDIENTS
1 orange
8 oz cranberries
1¼ cups sugar

orange

granulated sugar

cranberries

1 Pare the rind thinly from the orange, taking care not to remove any white pith. Squeeze the juice.

2 Place in a saucepan with the cranberries, sugar and ⅔ cup water.

3 Bring to a boil, stirring until the sugar has dissolved, then simmer for 10–15 minutes or until the berries burst.

4 Remove the rind and allow to cool before serving.

Mint Sauce

Tart, yet sweet, this simple sauce is the perfect foil to rich meat. It's best served, of course, with new season's roast lamb, but is wonderful, too, with grilled lamb chops or pan-fried duck.

Serves 6

INGREDIENTS
small bunch mint
1 tbsp sugar
2 tbsp boiling water
3 tbsp white wine vinegar

white wine vinegar

mint

sugar

1 Strip the leaves from the stalks.

2 Chop the leaves very finely.

3 Place in a bowl with the sugar and pour on the boiling water. Stir well and let stand for 5–10 minutes.

4 Add the vinegar and let stand for 1–2 hours before serving.

Tangy Orange Sauce
SAUCE BIGARADE

A tangy orange sauce for roast duck and rich game. For a full mellow flavour it is best made with the rich roasting-pan juices, but butter makes an admirable substitute if these aren't available.

Serves 4-6

INGREDIENTS

roasting pan juices or 25 g/1 oz/
  2 tbsp butter
40 g/1½ oz/3 tbsp plain flour
300 ml/½ pint/1¼ cups hot
  stock (preferably duck)
150 ml/¼ pint/ cup red wine
2 Seville oranges or 2 sweet
  oranges plus 2 tsp lemon juice
15 ml/1 tbsp orange-flavoured
  liqueur
30 ml/2 tbsp redcurrant jelly
salt and pepper

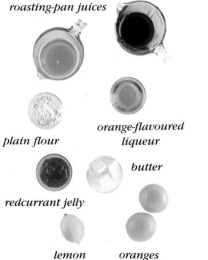

red wine

roasting-pan juices

plain flour

orange-flavoured liqueur

butter

redcurrant jelly

lemon   *oranges*

1 Pour off any excess fat from the roasting pan leaving the juices, or melt the butter in a small pan.

2 Sprinkle in the flour and cook, stirring continuously for 4 minutes or until lightly browned.

3 Off the heat, gradually blend in the hot stock and wine. Bring to the boil, stirring continuously. Lower the heat and simmer gently for 5 minutes.

4 Meanwhile, using a citrus zester, peel the rind thinly from one orange. Squeeze the juice from both oranges.

5 Blanch the rind; place it in a small pan, cover with water and bring to the boil. Cook for 5 minutes, drain and add the rind to the sauce.

6 Add the orange juice, liqueur and jelly to the sauce, stirring until the jelly has dissolved. Season to taste and pour over the jointed duckling or game.

Spicy Redcurrant Sauce

CUMBERLAND SAUCE

Spicy yet sweet, this redcurrant sauce is tailor-made for gammon and ham. A string of translucent, jewel-like redcurrants would make an excellent summery garnish for a dish served with this sauce.

Serves 8

INGREDIENTS
1 lemon
1 orange
2 sugar lumps
150 ml/¼ pint/ cup port
4 allspice berries
4 cloves
5 ml/1 tsp mustard seeds
225 g/8 oz redcurrant jelly
10 ml/2 tsp arrowroot
30 ml/2 tbsp orange liqueur
pinch of ground ginger

port

redcurrant jelly   *arrowroot*

lemon   *sugar lumps, cloves and allspice berries*

orange liqueur

ground ginger

orange

1 Peel the lemon thinly so that no white pith is removed. Cut into thin strips with a sharp knife or scissors, or peel the lemon with a citrus zester.

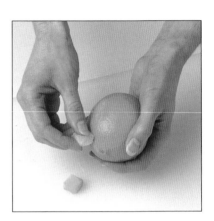

2 Blanch the rind; place in a small pan. Cover with water, bring to the boil, cook for 5 minutes, drain and reserve the rinds.

3 Wash the orange, then rub it all over with the sugar lumps until they are saturated with oil.

4 In a small pan bring the port, sugar lumps and whole spices to the boil. Remove from the heat and cool. Strain the port into a pan, add the jelly and stir over a low heat until dissolved.

COOK'S TIP
To develop a rich spicy flavour, store this sauce in the fridge for 2-3 days then bring to room temperature before serving.

5 Blend the arrowroot with the orange liqueur and stir into the sauce. Bring to the boil and cook for 1–2 minutes until it has thickened.

6 Remove from the heat and add the rinds and ground ginger to taste. Cool to room temperature before serving with hot or cold gammon slices or grilled lamb cutlets.

Mushroom and Wine Sauce

SAUCE CHASSEUR

This excellent sauce will transform simple pan-fried or grilled chicken and light meats into a dinner-party dish.

Serves 3-4

INGREDIENTS
25 g/1 oz/2 tbsp butter
1 shallot, finely chopped
115 g/4 oz button mushrooms, sliced
120 ml/4 fl oz/¹/₂ cup white wine
30 ml/2 tbsp brandy
1 quantity Sauce Espagnole (see page 30)
15 ml/1 tbsp chopped fresh tarragon or chervil

brandy

white wine

butter

shallot

button mushrooms

Sauce Espagnole

chervil

1 Melt the butter and fry the shallot until soft but not brown.

2 Add the mushrooms and sauté until they just begin to brown.

3 Pour in the wine and brandy, and simmer over a medium heat until reduced by half.

4 Add the Sauce Espagnole and herbs and heat through, stirring occasionally. Serve hot with grilled or roast pork, chicken or with rabbit.

COOK'S TIP
If you don't mind the grey tinge they give to the colour, flat mushrooms have more flavour than button ones.

Tartare Sauce

This is an authentic tartare sauce to serve with all kinds of fish, but for a simpler version you could always stir the flavourings into mayonnaise.

Serves 6

INGREDIENTS
2 hard-boiled eggs
1 egg yolk from a size 1 egg
10 ml/2 tsp lemon juice
175 ml/6 fl oz/¾ cup olive oil
5 ml/1 tsp chopped capers
5 ml/1 tsp chopped gherkin
5 ml/1 tsp chopped fresh chives
5 ml/1 tsp chopped fresh parsley
salt and pepper

chives

olive oil

hard-boiled eggs

lemon

parsley

gherkin and capers

egg yolk

1 Halve the hard-boiled eggs, remove the yolks and press them through a sieve into a bowl.

2 Blend in the raw yolk and mix until smooth. Stir in the lemon juice.

3 Add the oil very slowly, a little at a time, whisking constantly. When it begins to thicken, add the oil more quickly to form an emulsion.

4 Finely chop one egg white and stir into the sauce with the capers, gherkins and herbs. Season to taste. Serve as an accompaniment with fried or grilled fish.

Hollandaise Sauce

A rich butter sauce for fish and vegetables. The secret of success with this sauce is patience. Work in the butter slowly and thoroughly to give a thick, glossy texture.

Serves 2-3

INGREDIENTS
30 ml/2 tbsp white wine or
   tarragon vinegar
15 ml/1 tbsp water
6 black peppercorns
1 bay leaf
115 g/4 oz/$\frac{1}{2}$ cup butter
2 egg yolks
salt and pepper

bay leaf

egg yolks

black peppercorns

butter

white wine vinegar

1 Place the vinegar, water, peppercorns, and bay leaf in a saucepan. Simmer gently until the liquid has reduced by half. Strain and cool.

2 Cream the butter until soft.

3 In a double saucepan or a bowl sitting over a saucepan of gently simmering, but not boiling, water, whisk together the egg yolks and vinegar until light and fluffy.

4 Gradually add the butter a tiny piece at a time – about the size of a hazelnut will be enough. Whisk quickly until all the butter has been absorbed before adding any more.

5 Season lightly and, if the sauce is too sharp, add a little more butter.

6 For a thinner sauce stir in 1–2 tablespoons of single cream. Serve immediately with either steamed fish or fresh vegetables.

Rich Brown Sauce

SAUCE ESPAGNOLE

Espagnole is ideal for serving with red meat and game. It also makes a delicious full-flavoured base for other sauces, so make double quantity and keep some in the fridge.

Serves 4-6

INGREDIENTS
25 g/1 oz/2 tbsp butter
50 g/2 oz bacon pieces or streaky
    bacon, chopped
2 shallots, chopped
1 carrot, chopped
1 celery stick, chopped
mushroom trimmings (if
    available)
25 g/1 oz/2 tbsp plain flour
600 ml/1 pint/2¹/₂ cups hot
    Brown Stock
1 bouquet garni
30 ml/2 tbsp tomato purée
15 ml/1 tbsp sherry (optional)
salt and pepper

1 Melt the butter in a heavy-based saucepan and fry the bacon for 2–3 minutes. Add the vegetables and cook for a further 5–6 minutes until golden.

2 Stir in the flour and cook over a medium heat for 5–10 minutes until it has become a rich brown colour.

3 Remove from the heat and gradually blend in the stock.

brown stock

carrot

celery

mushroom trimmings

shallots

sherry

plain flour

butter

bouquet garni

tomato purée

bacon

4 Slowly bring to the boil continuing to stir until the sauce thickens. Add the bouquet garni, tomato purée and seasoning. Reduce the heat and simmer gently for one hour, stirring occasionally.

5 Strain the sauce, pressing the vegetables to extract the juice.

6 Skim off any fat with a metal spoon. Stir in the sherry and adjust the seasoning to taste. Serve with grilled lamb chops, or other red meat.

Creamy Madeira Sauce

NEWBURG SAUCE

This creamy Madeira-flavoured sauce will not mask delicate foods and is therefore ideal for shellfish. It also goes well with pan-fried chicken.

Serves 4

INGREDIENTS
15 g/¹/₂ oz/1 tbsp butter
1 small shallot, finely chopped
cayenne pepper
300 ml/¹/₂ pint/1¹/₄ cups double
  cream
60 ml/4 tbsp Madeira
salt and pepper
3 egg yolks

double cream

shallot   *egg yolks*

butter

cayenne   *Madeira*
pepper

1 Melt the butter in a double boiler or a bowl placed over a saucepan of simmering water. Cook the shallots until they are soft.

2 Add the cayenne and all but 60 ml/4 tbsp of the cream. Leave over the simmering water for 10 minutes to reduce slightly.

3 Stir in the Madeira.

4 Beat the yolks with the remaining cream and stir into the hot sauce. Continue stirring over barely simmering water until thickened. Season to taste. Spoon over seafood or chicken, reserving some for pouring, and serve immediately. Garnish with fresh herbs.

COOK'S TIP

For a luxurious festive look, stir in 15–30 ml/1–2 tbsp of pink or black lumpfish roe.

White Sauce

This basic recipe is wonderfully adaptable, but can be bland so always taste and season carefully.

Serves 6

INGREDIENTS
600 ml/1 pint/2¹/₂ cups milk
25 g/1 oz/2 tbsp plain flour
25 g/1 oz/2 tbsp butter
salt and pepper

plain flour

milk

butter

salt and pepper

VARIATIONS

PARSLEY SAUCE is traditionally served with bacon, fish and broad beans. Stir in 15 ml/2 tbsp finely chopped fresh parsley.

CHEESE SAUCE may be used for egg and vegetable gratins. Stir in 50 g/2 oz/¹/₂ cup finely grated mature Cheddar and 2.5 ml/¹/₂ tsp prepared mustard.

1 Warm the milk in a saucepan over a low heat, but do not boil.

2 In a separate saucepan melt the butter, then stir in the flour and cook gently for 1–2 minutes. Do not allow the roux to brown.

3 Off the heat, gradually blend in the milk, stirring vigorously after each addition to prevent lumps forming. Bring to the boil slowly and continue to stir all the time until the sauce thickens. Simmer gently for a further 3–4 minutes to thicken. Season to taste

COOK'S TIP
For a thicker, coating sauce, increase the amount of flour to 50 g/2 oz/¹/₂ cup and the butter to 50 g/2 oz/4 tbsp.

Béchamel Sauce

The creamy mellowness of the béchamel makes it ideal for lasagne as well as a base for many fish, egg and vegetable dishes.

Serves 4

INGREDIENTS
1 small onion
1 small carrot
1 celery stick
1 bouquet garni
6 black peppercorns
pinch freshly grated nutmeg or
    blade of mace
300 ml/¹/₂ pint/1¹/₄ cups milk
25 g/1 oz/2 tbsp butter
25 g/1 oz/2 tbsp plain flour
30 ml/2 tbsp single cream
salt and pepper

bouquet garni

butter

cream

*black peppercorns
and nutmeg*

onion

milk

plain flour

carrot

celery

COOK'S TIP
Flaked almonds or crisply fried buttered crumbs may be sprinkled over before serving for an added crunch.

1 Peel and finely chop the vegetables.

2 Put the milk, vegetables and flavourings in a saucepan. Bring to the boil. Remove from the heat, cover and allow to infuse for 30 minutes.

3 Melt the butter in a saucepan, remove from the heat and stir in the flour. Return to the heat and cook for 1–2 minutes.

4 Reheat the flavoured milk to almost boiling. Strain into a heat-proof jug, pressing the vegetables with the back of a spoon to extract the juices.

5 Off the heat gradually blend the milk into the roux, stirring vigorously after each addition.

6 Bring to the boil and stir continuously until the sauce thickens. Simmer gently for 3–4 minutes. Remove from the heat, adjust the seasoning to taste and stir in the cream.

Herby Butter Sauce

SAUCE BEARNAISE

For dedicated meat-eaters, this sauce adds a note of sophistication without swamping your grilled or pan-fried steak.

Serves 2-3

INGREDIENTS
45 ml/3 tbsp white wine vinegar
30 ml/2 tbsp water
1 small onion, finely chopped
a few fresh tarragon and chervil
  sprigs
1 bay leaf
6 crushed black peppercorns
115 g/4 oz/1/2 cup butter
2 egg yolks
15 ml/1 tbsp chopped fresh
  herbs, e.g. tarragon, parsley,
  chervil
salt and pepper

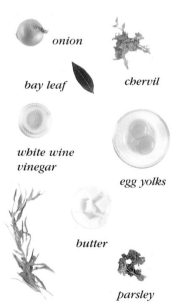

onion

bay leaf　　*chervil*

white wine vinegar

egg yolks

butter

parsley

tarragon

1 Place the vinegar, water, onion, herbs and peppercorns in a saucepan. Simmer gently until the liquor is reduced by half. Strain and cool.

2 Cream the butter until soft.

3 In a double saucepan or a bowl over a saucepan of gently simmering water, whisk the egg yolks and liquor until light and fluffy.

4 Gradually add the butter, half a teaspoonful at a time. Whisk until all the butter has been incorporated before adding any more.

5 Add the chopped herbs and season to taste.

6 Serve warm, not hot, on the side of a grilled steak or allow a good spoonful to melt over new potatoes.

Savoury Pouring Sauce

SAUCE VELOUTÉ

A smooth, velvety, sauce based on a white stock of fish, vegetable or meat. Choose whatever is suitable for the dish you are serving.

Serves 4

INGREDIENTS
600 ml/1 pint/2¹/₂ cups white
   stock
25 g/1 oz/2 tbsp butter
25 g/1 oz/2 tbsp plain flour
30 ml/2 tbsp single cream
salt and pepper

butter

white stock   *salt and pepper*

single cream

plain flour

1 Warm the stock but do not boil. In another pan melt the butter and stir in the flour. Cook over a moderate heat for 3–4 minutes until a pale, straw colour, stirring continuously.

2 Remove the pan from the heat and gradually blend in the stock. Return to the heat and bring to the boil, stirring continuously until the sauce thickens.

3 Continue to cook at a very slow simmer, stirring occasionally, until reduced by about a quarter.

4 Skim the surface during cooking or pour through a very fine strainer.

5 Just before serving, remove from the heat and stir in the cream. Season to taste.

Green Peppercorn Sauce

Green peppercorns in brine are a better choice than the dry-packed type because they give a more rounded flavour.

Serves 3-4

INGREDIENTS
15 ml/1 tbsp green peppercorns
  in brine, drained
1 small onion, finely chopped
25 g/1 oz/2 tbsp butter
300 ml/$\frac{1}{2}$ pint/$1\frac{1}{4}$ cups light
  stock
juice of $\frac{1}{2}$ lemon
15 ml/1 tbsp beurre manié
45 ml/3 tbsp double cream
5 ml/1 tsp Dijon mustard
salt and pepper

lemon

light stock

green peppercorns

onion

double cream

Dijon mustard

beurre manié

butter

1 Dry the peppercorns on absorbent kitchen paper, then crush lightly under the blade of a heavy-duty knife.

2 Soften the onion in the butter, add the stock and lemon juice and simmer for 15 minutes.

3 Whisk in the beurre manié a little at a time, and continue to cook until the sauce thickens.

4 Reduce the heat and stir in the peppercorns, cream and mustard. Season to taste. Serve hot with pork steaks and buttered pasta.

Barbecue Sauce

Brush this sauce liberally over chicken drumsticks, chops or kebabs before cooking on the barbecue, or serve as a hot or cold accompaniment to hot dogs and burgers.

Serves 4

INGREDIENTS

30 ml/2 tbsp vegetable oil
1 large onion, chopped
2 garlic cloves, crushed
400 g/14 oz can tomatoes
30 ml/2 tbsp Worcestershire sauce
15 ml/1 tbsp white wine vinegar
45 ml/3 tbsp honey
5 ml/1 tsp mustard powder
2.5 ml/¹/₂ tsp chilli seasoning or mild chilli powder
salt and pepper

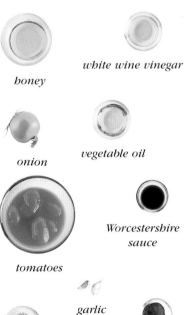

honey

white wine vinegar

onion

vegetable oil

tomatoes

Worcestershire sauce

garlic

mustard powder

mild chilli powder

1 Heat the oil and fry the onions and garlic until soft.

2 Stir in the remaining ingredients and simmer, uncovered, for 15–20 minutes stirring occasionally. Cool slightly.

3 Pour into a food processor or blender and process until smooth.

4 Press through a sieve if you prefer and adjust the seasoning.

Cider and Apple Cream

This sauce works excellently with grilled pork accompanied by its own garnish of rosy, glazed apple rings.

Serves 4

INGREDIENTS
40 g/1¹/₂ oz/3 tbsp butter
2 shallots, chopped
1 celery stick, chopped
1 carrot, chopped
25 g/1 oz/2 tbsp plain flour
450 ml/³/₄ pint/1⁷/₈ cup hot, light stock
300 ml/¹/₂ pint/1¹/₄ cups dry cider
60 ml/4 tbsp Calvados
60 ml/4 tbsp single cream
salt and pepper

FOR THE GLAZED APPLE RINGS
25 g/1 oz/2 tbsp butter
1 dessert apple, cored and sliced
1 tbsp granulated sugar

carrot

plain flour

butter

light stock   *shallots*

granulated sugar

celery

Calvados   *dessert apple*

single cream

dry cider

1 Melt the butter in a pan, add the shallots, celery and carrot. Cook over a gentle heat until soft but not coloured.

2 Sprinkle over the flour and cook over a low heat for 1–2 minutes, and make sure you stir continuously.

3 Remove the sauce from the heat and gradually blend in the stock, cider and Calvados.

4 Return to the heat and bring to the boil, stirring continuously until the sauce thickens. Then simmer, uncovered, until it is reduced by half.

5 Strain into a clean pan and add the cream. Heat through and taste before seasoning as it can be salty.

VARIATION
You could also use cider and apple cream sauce as an alternative to gravy with a traditional pork roast.

6 For the glazed apples, melt the butter in a frying pan. Add the apple slices in a single layer and sprinkle with sugar. Cook over a moderate heat, turning occasionally until soft and lightly caramelized. Serve the sauce with pan fried or grilled pork and veal, and garnish with the glazed apples.

Lemon and Tarragon Sauce

The sharpness of lemon and mild aniseed flavour of tarragon add zest to chicken, egg and steamed vegetable dishes.

Serves 4

INGREDIENTS
1 lemon
small bunch fresh tarragon
1 shallot, finely chopped
90 ml/6 tbsp white wine
1 quantity Velouté Sauce
45 ml/3 tbsp double cream
30 ml/2 tbsp brandy
salt and pepper

shallot

Velouté Sauce

tarragon

lemon

white wine

brandy

1 Thinly pare the rind from the lemon, taking care not to remove any white pith. Squeeze the juice into a pan.

2 Discard the coarse stalks from the tarragon. Chop the leaves and add all but 15 ml/1 tbsp to the pan with the lemon rind, shallot and wine.

COOK'S TIP

This sauce is an excellent accompaniment to pieces of boned chicken breast coverd with streaky bacon rashers and grilled or pan-fried.

3 Simmer gently until the liquid is reduced by half. Strain into a clean pan.

4 Add the Velouté Sauce, cream, brandy and reserved tarragon. Heat through, taste and adjust the seasoning if necessary.

Chinese-style Sweet and Sour Sauce

A great family favourite that adds a taste of the Orient.

Serves 4

INGREDIENTS
1 carrot
1 green pepper
15 ml/1 tbsp vegetable oil
1 small onion, chopped
1 garlic clove, crushed
2.5 cm/1 in piece root ginger,
  peeled and grated
15 ml/^{1}/$_2$ tbsp cornflour
300 ml/^{1}/$_2$ pint/1^1/$_4$ cups
  light stock
30 ml/2 tbsp tomato purée
15 g/^{1}/$_2$ oz/1 tbsp soft dark
  brown sugar
30 ml/2 tbsp white wine vinegar
30 ml/2 tbsp rice wine or sherry
salt and pepper
cucumber, to garnish

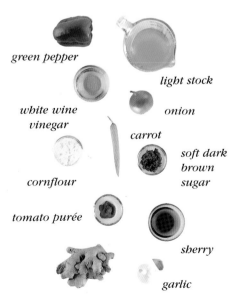

green pepper

white wine vinegar

light stock

onion

carrot

cornflour

soft dark brown sugar

tomato purée

sherry

garlic

root ginger

1 Peel the carrot and cut into matchstick-sized strips. Quarter the pepper, discard the stalks, seeds and membrane and cut into strips.

2 Heat the oil and fry the onion and garlic until soft but not brown. Add the carrot, pepper and ginger and cook for a further minute. Remove from the heat.

3 Blend the cornflour with a little stock and add to the vegetables, together with the remaining ingredients.

4 Stir over a moderate heat until the mixture boils and thickens. Simmer uncovered for 2–3 minutes until the vegetables are just tender. Adjust the seasoning and serve with strips of stir-fried pork or chicken and with rice or noodles.

Satay Dip

A deliciously pungent sauce which tastes great served with spicy chicken on skewers but is equally good as a dip for crisp vegetables.

Serves 6

INGREDIENTS
150 g/5 oz/1 cup roasted,
    unsalted peanuts
45 ml/3 tbsp vegetable oil
1 small onion, roughly chopped
2 garlic cloves, crushed
1 red chilli, seeded and chopped
2.5 cm/1 in piece root ginger,
    peeled and chopped
5 cm/2 in piece lemon grass,
    roughly chopped
2.5 ml/$^1/_2$ tsp ground cumin
45 ml/3 tbsp chopped fresh
    coriander stalks
15 ml/1 tbsp sesame oil
175 ml/6 fl oz/$^3/_4$ cup coconut milk
30 ml/2 tbsp thick soy sauce
    (kecap manis)
10 ml/2 tsp lime juice
salt and pepper
lime wedges and chives, to garnish

1 Rub the husks from the peanuts in a clean tea towel.

2 Grind to a smooth paste, with 30 ml/2 tbsp vegetable oil, in a blender or food processor. Set to one side.

garlic

red chilli

vegetable oil

limes

coconut milk

root ginger

thick soy sauce

onion

ground cumin

lemon grass

sesame oil

unsalted peanuts

coriander

3 Place the next seven ingredients in the blender or food processor and process to a fairly smooth paste.

4 Heat the remaining vegetable oil with the sesame oil in a small saucepan and add the onion paste. Cook over a low heat for about 10–15 minutes, stirring occasionally.

5 Stir in the peanuts, coconut milk, soy sauce and lime juice, and keep stirring while it heats through.

6 Adjust the seasoning, then pour into small bowls or saucers. Serve warm with grilled, skewered chicken or pork, or with small spicy meatballs, garnished with lime wedges and chives.

Creamy Dill and Mustard Sauce

This sauce will give a tangy, Scandinavian flavour to grilled fish dishes.

Serves 3-4

INGREDIENTS
25 g/1 oz/2 tbsp butter
20 g/³/₄ oz/1¹/₂ tbsp plain flour
300 ml/¹/₂ pint/1¹/₄ cups hot fish stock
15 ml/1 tbsp white wine vinegar
45 ml/3 tbsp chopped fresh dill
15 ml/1 tbsp wholegrain mustard
10 ml/2 tsp granulated sugar
2 egg yolks
salt and pepper

plain flour

granulated sugar

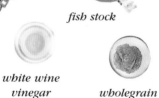

dill

fish stock

white wine vinegar

wholegrain mustard

egg yolks

butter

1 Melt the butter and stir in the flour. Cook for 1–2 minutes over a low heat, stirring continuously.

2 Remove from the heat and gradually blend in the hot stock. Return to the heat, bring to the boil, stirring all the time, then simmer for 2–3 minutes.

3 Remove from the heat and beat in the vinegar, dill, mustard and sugar.

4 Using a fork, beat the yolks in a small bowl and gradually add a small quantity of hot sauce. Return to the pan, whisking vigorously. Continue whisking over a very low heat for a further minute. Serve with grilled fillets of sole, plaice or brill.

Orange and Caper Sauce

A wonderfully sweet-sour sauce to add zest to otherwise plain white fish.

Serves 3-4

INGREDIENTS
25 g/1 oz/2 tbsp butter
1 onion, chopped
fish bones and trimmings
5 ml/1 tsp black peppercorns
300 ml/¹/₂ pint/1¹/₄ cups dry
    white wine
2 small oranges
15 ml/1 tbsp capers, drained
60 ml/4 tbsp crème fraîche
salt and pepper

fish bones and trimmings

onion

crème fraîche

dry white wine

butter

black peppercorns

capers

oranges

1 Melt the butter and add the onion. Sauté over a moderate heat until the onion is lightly browned.

2 Add the fish trimmings and peppercorns, and pour in the wine. Cover and simmer gently for 30 minutes.

3 Using a serrated knife, peel the oranges, ensuring all the white pith is removed. Ease the segments away from the membrane.

4 Strain the stock into a clean saucepan. Add the capers and orange segments together with any juice and heat through. Lower the heat and gently stir in the crème fraîche and seasoning. Serve hot with grilled or poached skate wings or plaice.

Watercress Cream

The delicate green colour of this cream sauce looks wonderful against pink-fleshed fish like salmon or salmon trout.

Serves 4

INGREDIENTS
2 bunches watercress
25 g/1 oz/2 tbsp butter
2 shallots, chopped
25 g/1 oz/2 tbsp plain flour
150 ml/¹/₄ pint/²/₃ cup hot fish stock
150 ml/¹/₄ pint/²/₃ cup dry white wine
5 ml/1 tsp anchovy essence
150 ml/¹/₄ pint/²/₃ cup single cream
salt
pinch cayenne pepper
lemon juice

anchovy essence

watercress

plain flour

shallots

cayenne pepper

single cream

dry white wine

fish stock

butter

1 Trim the watercress of any bruised leaves and coarse stalks. Blanch in boiling water for 5 minutes.

2 Drain and refresh the watercress under cold running water. In a sieve, press well with the back of a kitchen spoon to remove excess moisture then chop finely.

3 Melt the butter and fry the shallots until soft. Stir in the flour and cook for 1–2 minutes.

4 Turn off the heat and gradually blend in the stock, followed by the wine. Return to the heat, bring to the boil, stirring continuously, and simmer gently for 2–3 minutes.

VARIATION

To make rocket cream sauce, replace the watercress with 25 g/1 oz rocket leaves.

5 Strain into a clean pan, then add the watercress, anchovy essence and cream. Warm through over a low heat.

6 Season with salt and cayenne pepper and sharpen with lemon juice to taste. Serve immediately with grilled or poached salmon.

Garlic and Chilli Dip

This dip is delicious with fresh prawns and other shellfish. It will also spice up any kind of fish when used as an accompanying sauce.

Serves 4

INGREDIENTS
1 small red chilli
2.5 cm/1 in piece root ginger
2 garlic cloves
5 ml/1 tsp mustard powder
15 ml/1 tbsp chilli sauce
30 ml/2 tbsp olive oil
30 ml/2 tbsp light soy sauce
juice of two limes
30 ml/2 tbsp chopped fresh parsley
salt and pepper

mustard powder

parsley

red chilli

root ginger

light soy sauce

limes

chilli sauce

garlic

1 Halve the chilli, remove the seeds, stalk and membrane, and chop finely. Peel and roughly chop the ginger.

2 Crush the chilli, ginger, garlic and mustard powder to a paste, using a pestle and mortar.

3 In a bowl, mix together all the remaining ingredients, except the parsley. Add the paste and blend it in. Cover and chill for 24 hours.

4 Stir in the parsley and season to taste. It is best to serve in small individual bowls for dipping.

COOK'S TIP
Medium-sized Mediterranean prawns are ideal served with this sauce. Remove the shell but leave the tails intact so there is something to hold on to.

Saffron Cream

The subtle flavour and colouring of this sauce
marries well with steamed or pan-fried scallops in
a freshly-baked vol-au-vent.

Serves 4

INGREDIENTS
pinch saffron threads
30 ml/2 tbsp hot water
25 g/1 oz/2 tbsp butter
2 shallots, finely chopped
90 ml/6 tbsp dry white wine
60 ml/4 tbsp double cream
1 quantity fish Velouté Sauce, hot
2 egg yolks
salt and pepper
fresh chervil, to garnish

double cream   *egg yolks*

butter

Velouté Sauce

shallots

saffron threads

dry white wine

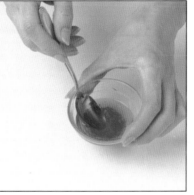

1 Soak the saffron threads in the water for 15 minutes.

2 Melt the butter and sauté the shallots until softened, add the wine and simmer gently until reduced by half.

3 Strain in the saffron water and add the cream, and cook very gently for about 2 minutes.

4 Blend the egg yolks with a little hot Velouté Sauce and, off the heat, whisk with the remaining sauce into the wine and cream. Season lightly.

Maître d'Hôtel Butter

Some fish have such a delicate flavour it's a pity to mask it with heavy sauces. This butter, and the variations below, make subtle accompaniments.

Serves 4-6

INGREDIENTS

115 g/4 oz/¹/₂ cup softened
    butter
30 ml/2 tbsp parsley, finely
    chopped
2.5 ml/¹/₂ tsp lemon juice
cayenne pepper
salt and pepper

parsley

lemon

cayenne pepper

butter

1 Beat the butter until creamy then beat in the parsley, lemon juice and cayenne pepper, and season lightly.

2 Spread the butter 1 cm/¹/₄ in thick on to aluminium foil, chill then cut into shapes with a knife or fancy cutter.

VARIATIONS

LEMON AND LIME BUTTER
Add 15 ml/1 tbsp finely grated lemon or lime rind and 15 ml/1 tbsp juice to the butter.

HERB BUTTER
eplace the parsley with 30 ml/2 tbsp chopped, mint, chives or tarragon.

GARLIC BUTTER
Add 2 skinned and crushed cloves of garlic to the softened butter with 15-30 ml/1-2 tbsp chopped parsley.

ANCHOVY BUTTER
Add 6 anchovy fillets, drained of oil and mashed with a fork, to the softened butter. Season with pepper only.

MUSTARD BUTTER
Add 10 ml/2 tsp English mustard and 30 ml/2 tbsp chopped chives to the butter.

3 Alternatively, form into a roll, wrap in clear film or aluminium foil and chil., Cut off slices as required.

COOK'S TIP
These butters will keep in the fridge for several days, and will also freeze, but make sure you wrap them well to avoid any loss of flavour.

Pesto Sauce

There is nothing more evocative of the warmth of Italy than a good home-made pesto. Serve generous spoonfuls with your favourite pasta.

Serves 3–4

INGREDIENTS
50 g/2 oz/2 cups tightly packed
    basil leaves
2 garlic cloves, crushed
30 ml/2 tbsp pine nuts
120 ml/4 fl oz/¹/₂ cup olive oil
40 g/1¹/₂ oz/²/₃ cup Parmesan
    cheese, finely grated
salt and pepper

garlic

Parmesan cheese

pine nuts

olive oil

basil

1 Using a pestle and mortar, grind the basil, garlic, pine nuts and seasoning to a fine paste.

2 Transfer the mixture to a bowl and whisk in the oil a little at a time.

3 Add the cheese and blend well. Adjust the seasoning to taste.

4 Alternatively, place the basil, garlic, pine nuts and seasoning in a food processor and grind as finely as possible.

5 With the food processor on, slowly add the oil in a thin stream to give a smooth paste.

6 Add the cheese and pulse quickly 3–4 times. Adjust the seasoning if necessary and heat gently.

VARIATION
Pesto also makes an excellent dressing on small new potatoes. Serve while still hot or allow to cool to room temperature.

Rich Tomato Sauce

For a full tomato flavour and rich red colour use only really ripe tomatoes. Fresh plum tomatoes are an excellent choice if you can find them.

Serves 4-6

INGREDIENTS

30 ml/2 tbsp olive oil
1 large onion, chopped
2 garlic cloves, crushed
1 carrot, finely chopped
1 celery stick, finely chopped
675 g/1^1/$_2$ lb tomatoes, peeled
    and chopped
150 ml/^{1}/$_4$ pint/^{2}/$_3$ cup red wine
150 ml/^{1}/$_4$ pint/^{2}/$_3$ cup vegetable
    stock
1 bouquet garni
15 ml/1 tbsp tomato purée
2.5-5 ml/^{1}/$_2$-1 tsp granulated
    sugar
salt and pepper

vegetable stock

onion

carrot

red wine

olive oil

garlic

tomato purée

tomatoes

celery

bouquet garni

1 Heat the oil and sauté the onion and garlic until soft. Add the carrot and celery and continue to cook, stirring occasionally, until golden.

2 Stir in the tomatoes, wine, stock, bouquet garni and seasoning. Bring to the boil, cover and simmer for 45 minutes, stirring occasionally.

3 Remove the bouquet garni and adjust the seasoning, adding sugar and tomato purée as necessary.

4 Serve the sauce as it is or, for a smoother texture, purée in a blender or food processor, or press through a sieve. Spoon over sliced courgettes or whole round beans.

Gorgonzola & Walnut Sauce

This is a very quick but indulgently creamy sauce. Serve with pasta and a green salad for a delicious lunch or supper.

Serves 2

INGREDIENTS

50 g/2 oz/4 tbsp butter
50 g/2 oz button mushrooms, sliced
150 g/5 oz Gorgonzola cheese
150 ml/¼ pint/⅔ cup soured cream
salt and pepper
25 g/1 oz Pecorino cheese, grated
50 g/2 oz/½ cup broken walnut pieces

soured cream

walnuts

button mushrooms

Pecorino cheese

Gorgonzola cheese

1 Melt the butter and gently fry the mushrooms until lightly browned.

2 With a fork, mash together the Gorgonzola, cream and seasoning.

3 Stir in the mushroom mixture and heat gently until melted.

4 Finally stir in the Pecorino cheese and the walnut pieces.

COOK'S TIP

For an impressive vegetable dish, layer with lightly cooked, thickly sliced potatoes. Sprinkle with more Pecorino cheese and bake at 180°C/350°F/Gas 4 for 1 hour.

Sweet Pepper & Chilli Sauce

A mellow, warming sauce, ideal with pasta. For a more extravagant supper dish add thickly sliced chorizo sausage with the sun-dried tomatoes.

Serves 3–4

INGREDIENTS
30 ml/2 tbsp olive oil
1 onion, chopped
1 garlic clove, crushed
2 large red or orange peppers, seeded and finely chopped
5 ml/1 tsp chilli seasoning
15 ml/1 tbsp paprika
2.5 ml/$\frac{1}{2}$ tsp dried thyme
1 x 225 g/8 oz can chopped tomatoes
300 ml/$\frac{1}{2}$ pint/1$\frac{1}{4}$ cups vegetable stock
2.5 ml/$\frac{1}{2}$ tsp granulated sugar
salt and pepper
30 ml/2 tbsp sun-dried tomatoes in oil, drained and chopped

onion

olive oil

garlic

red pepper

paprika

thyme

chopped tomatoes

sun-dried tomatoes

1 Heat the oil and sauté the onion, garlic and peppers for 4–5 minutes or until lightly browned.

2 Add the chilli, paprika and thyme and cook for a further minute.

3 Stir in the tomatoes, stock, sugar and seasoning, and bring to the boil. Cover and simmer for 30 minutes or until soft, adding more stock if necessary.

4 Ten minutes before the end of cooking, add the sun-dried tomatoes. Serve hot with freshly cooked pasta.

Spicy Tuna Dip

A piquant dip, delicious with breadsticks – use more oil for a sauce, less for filling hard-boiled eggs, tomatoes or celery sticks.

Serves 6

INGREDIENTS
1 x 90g/3^1/$_2$ oz can tuna fish in
  oil
olive oil
4 hard-boiled eggs
75 g/3 oz stoned green olives
1 x 50 g/2 oz can anchovy fillets,
  drained
45 ml/3 tbsp capers, drained
10 ml/2 tsp Dijon mustard
pepper
parsley, to garnish

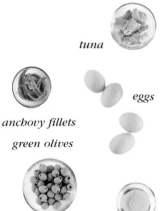

tuna

anchovy fillets

eggs

green olives

olive oil

Dijon mustard

1 Drain the tuna and make up the oil to 90 ml/6 tbsp with olive oil.

2 Halve the hard-boiled eggs, remove the yolks and then place in a blender or food processor. Discard the whites.

3 Reserve a few olives for garnishing, then add the rest to the blender together with the remaining ingredients. Whizz together until smooth. Season with pepper to taste.

4 Spoon into a bowl and garnish with the reserved olives and parsley. Serve with bread sticks for dipping.

Mousseline Sauce

A truly luscious sauce, subtly flavoured, rich and creamy.

Serves 4

INGREDIENTS
1 quantity Hollandaise sauce
or for a less rich sauce:
  2 egg yolks
  15 ml/1 tbsp lemon juice
  75 g/3 oz/6 tbsp softened
  butter
90 ml/6 tbsp double cream
salt and pepper

butter

egg yolks

lemon

double cream

1 If you are not using prepared Hollandaise, make the sauce; whisk the yolks and lemon juice in a bowl over a pan of barely simmering water until very thick and fluffy.

2 Whisk in the butter, but only a very little at a time, until it is thoroughly absorbed and the sauce has the consistency of mayonnaise.

3 Whisk the cream until stiff.

4 Fold into the warm Hollandaise or prepared sauce and adjust the seasoning. You can add a little more lemon juice for extra sharpness. Serve as a dip with prepared artichokes or artichoke hearts.

Creamy Gruyère Sauce

Gruyère gives this sauce a sweet nutty flavour and it melts wonderfully to a rich velvety smoothness.

Serves 6

INGREDIENTS

40 g/1½ oz/3 tbsp butter
40 g/1½ oz/3 tbsp plain flour
450 ml/¾ pint/1⅞ cup hot
  vegetable or light stock
2 egg yolks
5 ml/1 tsp Dijon mustard
pinch of ground mace
30 ml/2 tbsp dry sherry
75 g/3 oz Gruyère cheese, grated

vegetable stock

dry sherry

ground mace

Gruyère cheese   *butter*

egg yolks   *plain flour*

Dijon mustard

1 Melt the butter and stir in the flour, and cook over a moderate heat for about 1–2 minutes.

2 Remove from the heat and gradually blend in the hot stock. Return to the heat and bring to the boil, stirring continuously until the sauce thickens. Simmer gently for 3–4 minutes.

3 In a small bowl, blend the egg yolks with a little hot sauce.

4 Return to the pan and cook over a very low heat for 1–2 minutes. Do not allow to boil. Finally stir in the flavourings and cheese. Season to taste. Serve with steamed broccoli, cauliflower or leeks.

COOK'S TIP

Crisply fried buttered crumbs and flaked or nibbed almonds may be sprinkled over for added crunch.

MARINADES

Red Wine and Juniper Marinade

Marinating develops a rich base for casseroles
and stews. This marinade is also excellent for
pot-roasted beef.

Serves 4-6

INGREDIENTS
700 g/1¹/₂ lb boned leg of lamb,
  trimmed and cut into 2.5 cm/
  1 in cubes

FOR THE MARINADE:
2 carrots, cut into batons
225 g/8 oz baby onions or
  shallots
100 g/4 oz button mushrooms
4 rosemary sprigs
8 juniper berries, lightly crushed
8 black peppercorns, lightly
  crushed
300 ml/¹/₂ pint/1¹/₄ cups red
  wine
30 ml/2 tbsp vegetable oil
150 ml/¹/₄ pint/²/₃ cup stock
30 ml/2 tbsp beurre manié

1 Place the meat in a bowl, add the vegetables, rosemary and spices then pour over the wine. Cover and leave in a cool place for 4-5 hours, stirring once or twice during this time.

2 Remove the lamb and vegetables with a slotted spoon and set aside. Strain the marinade into a jug.

3 Preheat the oven to 170°C/325°F/Gas 3. Heat the oil in a pan and fry the meat and vegetables in batches until lightly browned. Pour over the reserved marinade and stock. Cover and cook in the oven for 2 hours.

baby onions   red wine

juniper berries   button
and black   mushrooms
peppercorns

rosemary   carrot

4 Twenty minutes before the end of cooking stir in the beurre manié, cover and return to the oven. Season to taste before serving.

Chinese-style Marinade with Toasted Sesame Seeds

Toasted sesame seeds bring their distinctive smoky aroma to this Oriental marinade.

Serves 4

INGREDIENTS
450 g/1 lb rump steak
30 ml/2 tbsp sesame seeds
15 ml/1 tbsp sesame oil
30 ml/2 tbsp vegetable oil
100 g/4 oz small mushrooms, quartered
1 large green pepper, seeded and diced
4 spring onions, chopped diagonally

FOR THE MARINADE:
10 ml/2 tsp cornflour
30 ml/2 tbsp rice wine or sherry
15 ml/1 tbsp lemon juice
15 ml/1 tbsp soy sauce
few drops Tabasco sauce
2.5 cm/1 in piece root ginger, peeled and grated
1 garlic clove, crushed

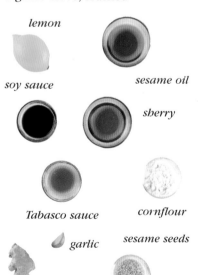

lemon

soy sauce

sesame oil

sherry

Tabasco sauce

cornflour

garlic

sesame seeds

root ginger

1 Trim the steak and cut into thin strips about 1 cm × 5 cm/½ × 2 in.

2 In a bowl, blend the cornflour with the sherry then stir in the other marinade ingredients. Stir in the beef strips, cover and leave in a cool place for 3-4 hours.

3 Place the sesame seeds in a large frying pan or wok. Cook dry over a moderate heat, shaking the pan until the seeds are golden. Reserve on one side.

4 Heat the oils in the frying pan. Drain the beef, reserving the marinade, and brown a few pieces at a time. Remove with a slotted spoon.

VARIATION
This marinade would also be good with pork or chicken.

5 Add the mushrooms and pepper and fry for 2–3 minutes, moving the vegetables continuously. Add the spring onions and cook for a further minute.

6 Return the beef with the marinade and stir over a moderate heat for a further 2 minutes until the ingredients are evenly coated with glaze. Just before serving, sprinkle with sesame seeds.

Summer Herb Marinade

Make the best use of summer herbs in this marinade, which is designed for the barbecue. Any combination may be used depending on what you have to hand, and it can be used with veal, chicken, pork, salmon or lamb.

Serves 4

INGREDIENTS
4 pieces of meat or fish

FOR THE MARINADE:
fresh herb sprigs, e.g. chervil,
 thyme, parsley, sage, chives,
 rosemary, oregano
90 ml/6 tbsp olive oil
45 ml/3 tbsp tarragon vinegar
1 garlic clove, crushed
2 spring onions, chopped
salt and pepper

parsley

chervil

garlic

tarragon vinegar

olive oil

spring onions

chives

thyme

rosemary

oregano

I Discard any coarse stalks or damaged leaves from the herbs, then chop very finely.

2 Mix the herbs with the remaining marinade ingredients.

3 Place the meat or fish in a bowl and pour over the marinade. Cover and leave in a cool place for 4–6 hours.

4 Brush the pieces of meat or fish with the marinade and cook under a hot grill or over a barbecue, turning occasionally until they are tender. Baste with the marinade while they cook. Serve garnished with fresh herbs.

Ginger and Lime Marinade

This fragrant marinade will guarantee a mouth-watering aroma from the barbecue, and is as delicious with chicken or pork as it is with fish.

Serves 4-6

INGREDIENTS
FOR THE KEBABS:
500 g/1¼ lb prawns and cubed
 monkfish
selection of prepared vegetables,
 e.g. red, green or orange
 peppers, courgettes, button
 mushrooms, red onion, bay
 leaves, cherry tomtoes

FOR THE MARINADE:
3 limes
15 ml/1 tbsp green cardamom
 pods
1 onion, finely chopped
2.5 cm/1 in piece root ginger,
 peeled and grated
1 large garlic clove,crushed
45 ml/3 tbsp olive oil

limes

olive oil

root ginger

green cardamoms

onion

garlic

1 Finely grate the rind from one lime and squeeze the juice from all of them.

2 Split the cardamom pods and remove the seeds. Crush with a pestle and mortar or the back of a heavy-bladed knife.

3 Mix all the marinade ingredients together and pour over the meat or fish. Stir in gently, cover and leave in a cool place for 2–3 hours.

4 Thread four skewers alternately with fish and vegetables. Cook slowly under a hot grill or over a barbecue, basting occasionally with the marinade.

Spicy Yogurt Marinade

Plan this dish well in advance; the extra-long marinating time is necessary to develop a really mellow spicy flavour.

VARIATION
This marinade will also work well brushed over skewers of lamb or pork fillet.

Serves 6

INGREDIENTS
6 chicken pieces
juice of 1 lemon
5 ml/1 tsp salt

FOR THE MARINADE:
5 ml/1 tsp coriander seeds
10 ml/2 tsp cumin seeds
6 cloves
2 bay leaves
1 onion, quartered
2 garlic cloves
5 cm/2 in piece root ginger, peeled and roughly chopped
2.5 ml/^{1}/$_2$ tsp chilli powder
5 ml/1 tsp turmeric
150 ml/^{1}/$_4$ pint/^{2}/$_3$ cup natural yogurt
lemon, lime or coriander, to garnish

lemon

yogurt

coriander seeds

root ginger

onion

garlic

bay leaves

chilli powder

turmeric

cloves

cumin seeds

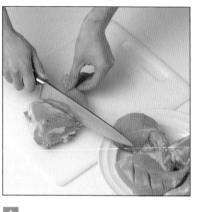

1 Skin the chicken joints and make deep slashes in the fleshiest parts with a sharp knife. Sprinkle over the lemon and salt and rub in.

2 Spread the coriander and cumin seeds, cloves and bay leaves in the bottom of a large frying pan and dry-fry over a moderate heat until the bay leaves are crispy.

3 Cool the spices and grind coarsely with a pestle and mortar.

4 Finely mince the onion, garlic and ginger in a food processor or blender. Add the ground spices, chilli, turmeric and yogurt, then strain in the lemon juice from the chicken.

5 Arrange the chicken in a single layer in a roasting tin. Pour over the marinade, then cover and chill for 24–36 hours.

6 Occasionally turn the chicken pieces in the marinade. Preheat the oven to 200°C/400°F/Gas 6. Cook the chicken for 45 minutes. Serve hot or cold, garnished with fresh leaves and slices of lemon or lime.

Winter Spiced Ale Marinade

Serve this on frosty evenings with buttered swede and crisply cooked cabbage. This marinade can also be used in a casserole of beef or lamb pieces.

Serves 6

INGREDIENTS
1.4 kg/3 lb top rump beef

FOR THE MARINADE:
1 onion, sliced
2 carrots, sliced
2 celery sticks, sliced
2–3 parsley stalks, lightly crushed
large fresh thyme sprig
2 bay leaves
6 cloves, lightly crushed
1 cinnamon stick
8 black peppercorns
300 ml/$\frac{1}{2}$ pint/$1\frac{1}{4}$ ale
45 ml/3 tbsp vegetable oil
30 ml/2 tbsp beurre manié
salt and pepper

carrot

parsley

vegetable oil

beurre manié

cinnamon

cloves and black peppercorns

thyme

onion

brown ale

bay leaves

celery

1 Place the meat in a polythene bag placed inside a large deep bowl. Add the vegetables, herbs and spices, then pour over the ale. Seal the bag and leave in a cool place for 5–6 hours.

2 Remove the beef and set aside. Strain the marinade into a bowl, reserving the vegetables.

3 Heat the oil in a flame-proof casserole. Fry the vegetables until lightly browned, then remove with a slotted spoon and set aside. Brown the beef all over in the remaining oil.

4 Preheat the oven to 170°C/ 325°F/ Gas 3. Pour over the reserved marinade and return the vegetables to the casserole. Cover the casserole and cook for 2$\frac{1}{2}$ hours. Turn the beef 2 or 3 times in the marinade during this time.

5 To serve, remove the beef and slice neatly. Arrange on a plate with the vegetables. Stir the beurre manié into the marinade and bring to the boil. Adjust the seasoning before serving.

Lemon and Rosemary

If you are serving lamb for your Sunday roast, marinate overnight in the fridge.

Serves 6

INGREDIENTS
1.5 kg/3–3½ lb leg of lamb
2 garlic cloves, sliced

FOR THE MARINADE:
1 lemon, sliced
6 rosemary sprigs
4 lemon thyme sprigs
300 ml/½ pint/1¼ cups dry
    white wine
60 ml/4 tbsp olive oil
salt and pepper
15 ml/1 tbsp cornflour

rosemary

lemon thyme

lemon

olive oil

dry white wine

garlic

1 Make small cuts over the surface of the lamb and insert a slice of garlic in each, so they sit proud.

2 Place the lamb in a roasting tin, with the lemon slices and herbs scattered over it. Mix the remaining marinade ingredients and pour over the joint. Cover and leave in a cool place for 4–6 hours, turning occasionally. Preheat the oven to 180°C/350°F/Gas 4. Roast the lamb for 25 minutes per 450 g/1 lb plus 25 minutes over.

3 When the lamb is cooked, transfer to a warmed plate to rest. Drain the excess fat from the pan. Blend the cornflour with a little cold water and stir into the juices, stir over a moderate heat for 2–3 minutes and season to taste.

VARIATION

You can also use lemon and rosemary marinade for chicken pieces, but you must roast the meat without the marinade because otherwise it will become tough. Use the marinade for making into gravy when the chicken is cooked.

Orange and Green Peppercorn

This is an excellent light marinade for whole fish. The mouth-watering beauty of a whole fish and the soft-coloured marinade needs only a sprig of fresh herb to garnish.

Serves 4

INGREDIENTS
1 medium-sized whole fish, e.g. salmon trout, bass or sea bream, cleaned

FOR THE MARINADE:
1 red onion
2 small oranges
90 ml/6 tbsp light olive oil
30 ml/2 tbsp cider vinegar
30 ml/2 tbsp green peppercorns in brine, drained
30 ml/2 tbsp chopped fresh parsley
salt and sugar

oranges

red onion

cider vinegar

parsley

green peppercorns

light olive oil

1 With a sharp knife, slash the fish 3–4 times on both sides.

2 Line an ovenproof dish with foil. Peel and slice the onion and oranges. Lay half in the bottom of the dish, place the fish on top, and cover with the remaining onion and orange.

3 Mix the remaining marinade ingredients and pour over the fish. Cover and stand for 4 hours, occasionally spooning the marinade over the top.

4 Preheat the oven to 180°C/350°F/Gas 4. Fold up the aluminium foil over the fish and seal loosely. Bake for 15 minutes per 450 g/1 lb, plus 15 minutes over.

Tomato Salsas

Salsa is Spanish for sauce, but elsewhere it has come to mean a side dish of finely chopped vegetables or fruits, which really enhances the meals it accompanies.

Serves 6

INGREDIENTS
6 medium tomatoes
1 green Kenyan chilli
2 spring onions, chopped
10 cm/4 in length cucumber,
   diced
30 ml/2 tbsp lemon juice
30 ml/2 tbsp fresh coriander,
   chopped
15 ml/1 tbsp fresh parsley,
   chopped
salt and pepper

tomatoes
basil
orange pepper
parsley
lemon
spring onions
coriander *garlic*
cucumber *capers*
green Kenyan chilli

1 Cut a small cross in the stalk end of each tomato. Place in a bowl and cover with boiling water.

2 After 30 seconds or as soon as the skins split, drain and plunge into cold water. Gently slide off the skins. Quarter the tomatoes, remove the seeds and dice the flesh.

3 Halve the chilli, remove the stalk, seeds and membrane, and chop finely.

4 Mix together all the ingredients and transfer to a serving bowl. Chill for 1–2 hours before serving.

VARIATIONS

Tomato and Caper Salsa:
Prepare the tomatoes and stir in
the onion and lemon juice. Add
six torn sprigs of basil and 15
ml/1 tbsp roughly chopped
capers. Season to taste.

Tomato and Roast Pepper Salsa:
Prepare 4 tomatoes and stir in the
chilli, onion and herbs. Add a
roasted, peeled and diced orange
pepper and a crushed garlic
clove. Season to taste.

Cool Mint Raita

The ideal antidote to any spicy food, especially fiery Indian curries.

Serves 4

INGREDIENTS
6 large mint sprigs
1 small onion
$^{1}/_{2}$ cucumber
300 ml/$^{1}/_{2}$ pint/1$^{1}/_{4}$ cups natural
    yogurt
2.5 ml/$^{1}/_{2}$ tsp salt
2.5 ml/$^{1}/_{2}$ tsp sugar
pinch chilli powder
mint sprig, to garnish

chilli powder

mint

onion

cucumber

yogurt

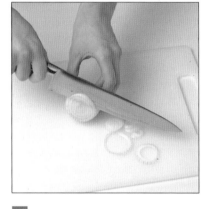

1 Tear the mint leaves from their stalks and chop finely.

2 Peel and very thinly slice the onion, separating it into rings. Cut the cucumber into 5 mm/$^{1}/_{4}$ in dice.

3 Mix together the mint, onion, cucumber, yogurt, salt and sugar. Spoon into a serving bowl and chill.

4 Just before serving sprinkle with chilli powder and garnish with mint.

VARIATION
This also makes a deliciously fresh dip for crudites, for a creamier texture use Greek yogurt, and add some crushed garlic for extra flavour. Serve with fresh vegetables or tortilla chips.

Guacamole

Avocados discolour quickly so make this sauce just before serving. If you do need to keep it for any length of time, cover closely with clear film and chill in the fridge.

Serves 6

INGREDIENTS
2 large ripe avocados
1 small onion, finely chopped
1 garlic clove, crushed
2 tomatoes
juice of half a lemon
15 ml/1 tbsp olive oil
pinch ground coriander
few drops of Tabasco sauce
salt and pepper
pinch of cayenne pepper

ground coriander

tomatoes

olive oil

onion

Tabasco sauce

lemon

avocados

cayenne pepper

1 Halve the avocados, remove the stones and scoop out the flesh into a large bowl.

2 Using a fork, mash together with the onion and garlic until smooth.

3 Peel the tomatoes (as for Tomato Salsa), remove the seeds and chop finely. Stir into the avocado mixture with the lemon juice and oil.

4 Season to taste with coriander, Tabasco sauce, salt and pepper. Spoon into small bowls and sprinkle with cayenne pepper. Serve with corn chips and crisp vegetables or serve as a sauce with chilli and hot tortillas.

Chilli and Coconut Salsa

A sweet-sour salsa that goes well with grilled or barbecued fish.

Serves 6-8

INGREDIENTS
1 small coconut
1 small pineapple
2 green Kenyan chillies
5 cm/2 in piece lemon grass
60 ml/4 tbsp natural yogurt
2.5 ml/½ tsp salt
30 ml/2 tbsp chopped coriander
coriander sprigs, to garnish

coconut

green chillies

lemon grass

pineapple

yogurt

coriander

1 Puncture two of the coconut eyes with a screwdriver and drain the milk out from the shell.

2 Crack the shell, prise away the flesh, and coarsely grate the coconut into a bowl.

3 Cut the rind from the pineapple with a sharp knife and remove the eyes with a potato peeler. Finely chop the flesh and add to the coconut together with any juice.

4 Halve the chillies lengthways and remove the stalks, seeds and membrane. Chop very finely and stir into the coconut mixture.

5 Finely chop the lemon grass with a very sharp knife. Add to the coconut mixture and stir in.

6 Add the remaining ingredients and stir well. Spoon into a serving dish and garnish with coriander sprigs.

Roasted Pepper and Ginger Salsa

Char-grilling to remove the skins will take away any bitterness from the peppers.

Serves 6

VARIATION
For a spicier version of this recipe, add a green chilli, finely chopped, to the pestle and mortar when grinding the ginger and garlic. Or simply add a sprinkle of cayenne pepper to the finished dish before chilling.

INGREDIENTS
1 large red pepper
1 large yellow pepper
1 large orange pepper
2.5 cm/1 in piece root ginger
2.5 ml/$^1/_2$ tsp coriander seeds
5 ml/1 tsp cumin seeds
1 small garlic clove
30 ml/2 tbsp lime or lemon juice
1 small red onion, finely chopped
30 ml/2 tbsp chopped fresh coriander
5 ml/1 tsp chopped fresh thyme
salt and pepper

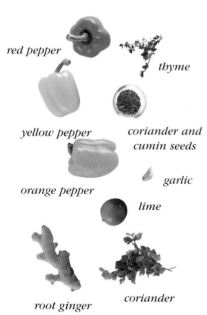

red pepper

thyme

yellow pepper

coriander and cumin seeds

garlic

orange pepper

lime

root ginger

coriander

1 Quarter the peppers and remove the stalk, seeds and membranes.

2 Grill the quarters, skin side up, until charred and blistered. Rub away the skins and slice very finely.

3 Peel or scrape the root ginger and chop roughly.

4 Over a moderate heat, gently dry-fry the spices for 30 seconds to 1 minute, making sure they don't scorch.

5 Crush the spices in a pestle and mortar. Add the ginger and garlic and continue to work to a pulp. Work in the lime or lemon juice.

6 Mix together the peppers, spice mixture, onion and herbs. Season to taste and spoon into a serving bowl. Chill for 1–2 hours before serving as an accompaniment to barbecued meats or Halloumi cheese kebabs.

Crème Anglais

Here is the classic English custard, light, creamy and delicious - far superior to packet versions. Serve hot or cold.

Serves 4

INGREDIENTS
1 vanilla pod
450ml/³/₄ pint/1⁷/₈ cups milk
40 g/1¹/₂ oz/3 tbsp caster sugar
4 egg yolks

vanilla pod

milk

eggs

caster sugar

1 Split the vanilla pod and place in a saucepan with the milk. Bring slowly to the boil. Remove from the heat, then cover and infuse for 10 minutes before removing the pod.

2 Beat together the sugar and egg yolk until thick, light and creamy.

VARIATION
Infuse a few strips of thinly pared lemon or orange rind with the milk, instead of the vanilla pod.

COOK'S TIP
To help prevent curdling, blend 5 ml/1 tsp of cornflour with the egg yolks and sugar.

3 Slowly pour the warm milk on to the egg mixture, stirring constantly.

4 Transfer to the top of a double boiler or place the bowl over a saucepan of hot water. Stir constantly over a low heat for 10 minutes or until the mixture coats the back of the spoon. Remove from the heat immediately as curdling will occur if the custard is allowed to simmer.

5 Strain the custard into a jug if serving hot or, if serving cold, strain into a bowl and cover the surface with buttered paper or clear film.

Chocolate Fudge Sauce

A real treat if you're not counting calories. Fabulous
with scoops of vanilla ice-cream.

Serves 6

INGREDIENTS
150 ml/¹/₄ pint/²/₃ cup double
    cream
50 g/2 oz/4 tbsp butter
50 g/2 oz/¹/₄ cup vanilla sugar
175 g/6 oz plain chocolate
30 ml/2 tbsp brandy

VARIATIONS

White Chocolate and Orange
Sauce:
40 g/1¹/₂ oz/3 tbsp caster sugar,
    to replace vanilla sugar
175 g/6 oz white chocolate, to
    replace plain chocolate
30 ml/2 tbsp orange liqueur, to
    replace brandy
finely grated rind of 1 orange

Coffee Chocolate Fudge:
50 g/2 oz/¹/₄ cup light brown
    sugar, to replace vanilla sugar
30 ml/2 tbsp coffee liqueur or
    dark rum, to replace brandy
15 ml/1 tbsp coffee essence

vanilla sugar

brandy

plain chocolate

butter

double cream

1 Heat the cream with the butter
and sugar in the top of a double boiler
or in a bowl over a saucepan of hot
water. Stir until smooth, then cool

2 Break the chocolate into the
cream. Stir until it is melted and
thoroughly combined.

3 Stir in the brandy a little at a time,
then cool to room temperature.

4 For the White Chocolate and
Orange Sauce, heat the cream and
butter with the sugar and orange rind in
the top of a double boiler, until
dissolved. Then, follow the recipe to the
end, but using white chocolate and
orange liqueur instead.

5 For the Coffee Chocolate Fudge,
follow the recipe, using light brown
sugar and coffee liqueur or rum. Stir in
the coffee essence at the end.

6 Serve the sauce over cream-filled
profiteroles, and serve any that is
leftover separately.

Ginger and Honey Syrup

Particularly good for winter puddings, this sauce can be served hot or cold.

Serves 4

INGREDIENTS
1 lemon
4 green cardamom pods
1 cinnamon stick
150 ml/^{1}/$_4$ pint/^{2}/$_3$ cup runny honey
30 ml/2 tbsp ginger syrup, from the jar
3 pieces stem ginger

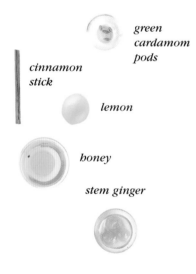

green cardamom pods

cinnamon stick

lemon

honey

stem ginger

1 Thinly pare 2 strips of rind from the lemon with a potato peeler.

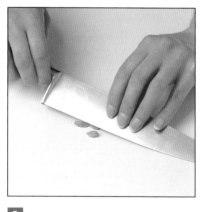

2 Lightly crush the cardamom pods with the back of a heavy-bladed knife.

3 Place the lemon rind, cardamom, cinnamon stick, honey and ginger syrup in a heavy-based saucepan with 60 ml/4 tbsp water. Bring to the boil and simmer for 2 minutes.

4 Chop the ginger and stir into the sauce with the juice of half the lemon. Pour over a winter fruit salad of poached dried fruits and sliced oranges. Chill to serve.

VARIATION
To serve hot with steamed puddings, strain at the end of step 3 before stirring in the stem ginger and lemon.

Sabayon

Serve this frothy sauce hot over steamed puddings or chill as shown and serve just as it is with light dessert biscuits or whatever you prefer. Never let it stand, as it will collapse.

Serves 4-6

INGREDIENTS
1 egg
2 egg yolks
75 g/3 oz/²/₃ cup caster sugar
150 ml/1/4 pint/²/₃ cup sweet
  white wine
finely grated rind and juice of
  1 lemon

lemon

sweet white wine

egg yolks

eggs

caster sugar

1 Whisk the egg, yolks and sugar until they are pale and thick.

2 Stand the bowl over a saucepan of hot – not boiling – water. Add the wine and lemon juice, a little at a time, whisking vigorously.

3 Continue whisking until the mixture is thick enough to leave a trail. Whisk in the lemon rind. If serving hot serve immediately over pudding or fruit salad.

4 To serve cold, place over a bowl of iced water and whisk until chilled. Pour into small glasses and serve at once.

COOK'S TIP
A generous pinch of arrowroot whisked together with the egg yolks and sugar will prevent the sauce collapsing too quickly.

Butterscotch Sauce

A deliciously sweet sauce which will be loved by adults and children alike! Serve with ice-cream or with pancakes or waffles.

Serves 4-6

INGREDIENTS
75 g/3 oz/¹/₃ cup butter
175 g/6 oz/³/₄ cup soft dark brown sugar
175 ml/6 fl oz/³/₄ cup evaporated milk
50 g/2 oz/¹/₂ cup hazelnuts

soft dark brown sugar

evaporated milk

hazelnuts

butter

1 Melt the butter and sugar in a heavy-based pan, bring to the boil and boil for 2 minutes. Cool for 5 minutes.

2 Heat the evaporated milk to just below boiling point, then gradually stir into the sugar mixture. Cook over a low heat for 2 minutes, stirring frequently.

3 Spread the hazelnuts on a baking sheet and toast under a hot grill.

4 Tip on to a clean tea towel and rub briskly to remove the skins.

5 Chop the nuts roughly and stir into the sauce. Serve hot, poured over scoops of vanilla ice-cream and warm waffles or pancakes.

VARIATION

Substitute any nut for the hazelnuts, pecans, for example, add a luxurious flavour. You could also add plump, juicy raisins and a dash of rum instead of the nuts.

Redcurrant and Raspberry Coulis

A dessert sauce for the height of summer to serve with light meringues and fruit sorbets. Make it particularly pretty with a decoration of fresh flowers and leaves.

Serves 6

INGREDIENTS
225 g/8 oz redcurrants
450 g/1 lb raspberries
50 g/2 oz/¼ cup icing sugar
15 ml/1 tbsp cornflour
juice of 1 orange
30 ml/2 tbsp double cream

orange

icing sugar

double cream

cornflour

redcurrants and raspberries

1 Strip the redcurrants from their stalks using a fork. Place in a food processor or blender with the raspberries and sugar, and purée until it is smooth.

2 Press the mixture through a fine sieve into a bowl and discard the seeds and pulp.

3 Blend the cornflour with the orange juice then stir into the fruit purée. Transfer to a saucepan and bring to the boil, stirring continuously, and cook for 1–2 minutes until smooth and thick. Leave until cold.

4 Spoon the sauce over each plate. Drip the cream from a teaspoon to make small dots evenly around the edge. Draw a cocktail stick through the dots to form heart shapes. Scoop or spoon sorbet into the middle and decorate with flowers.

Lemon and Lime Sauce

A tangy, refreshing sauce to end a heavy meal, it goes well with pancakes or fruit tarts.

Serves 4

INGREDIENTS
1 lemon
2 limes
50 g/2 oz/¼ cup caster sugar
25 ml/1½ tbsp arrowroot
300 ml/½ pint/1¼ cups water
lemon balm or mint, to garnish

limes

arrowroot

caster sugar

lemon

1 Using a citrus zester, peel the rinds thinly from the lemon and limes. Squeeze the juice from the fruit.

2 Place the rind in a pan, cover with water and bring to the boil. Drain through a sieve and reserve the rind.

3 In a small bowl, mix a little sugar with the arrowroot. Blend in enough water to give a smooth paste. Heat the remaining water, pour in the arrowroot, and stir continuously until the sauce boils and thickens.

4 Stir in the remaining sugar, citrus juice and reserved rind, and serve hot with freshly made pancakes. Decorate with lemon balm or mint.

VARIATION
This sauce can also be made with orange and lemon rind if you prefer, and makes an ideal accompaniment for a rich orange or mandarin cheesecake.

Brandy Butter

Traditionally served with Christmas pudding and mince pies, but a good spoonful on a hot baked apple is equally delicious.

Serves 6

INGREDIENTS

100 g/4 oz/¹/₂ cup butter
100 g/4 oz/¹/₂ cup icing, caster or
    soft light brown sugar
45 ml/3 tbsp brandy

butter

soft light
brown sugar

brandy

1 Cream the butter until very pale and soft.

2 Beat in the sugar gradually.

3 Add the brandy, a few drops at a time, beating continuously. Add enough for a good flavour but take care it does not curdle.

4 Pile into a small serving dish and allow to harden. Alternatively, spread on to aluminium foil and chill until firm. Cut into shapes with small fancy cutters.

VARIATION

Cumberland Rum Butter
Use soft light brown sugar and rum instead of brandy. Beat in the grated rind of 1 orange and a good pinch of mixed spice with the sugar.